This book is designed for your pleasure and reference.

Once you purchase this book - feel free to make notes in it, make lists in it, write in it - whatever you like.

This Grandpa book belongs to:

_____

From: _____

Date Received: _____

Grandpa Told Me...

things your father meant to tell you.

Grandpa Told Me...
things your father meant to tell you.

by Joe Baker

Fourth Edition
completely revised
Joe Baker & Associates, Inc. - Publishing Division

Independence, Missouri

Grandpa Told Me...things your father meant to tell you.
by Joe Baker

Fourth edition: 2008 revised
Third edition: 1997 revised
Second edition: 1990 revised
First edition: 1989

Contact: Joe Baker & Associates, Inc.
               Publishing Division
               539 Tennessee Avenue
               Independence, MO 64053-1134
               816-254-1212
               Web site: joebakerandassociates.com

Bibliography:
Includes Table of Contents

ISBN: 978-0-9817545-2-9

Published by Joe Baker & Associates, Inc.
Book Cover Design by Stephen Rogers Baker

Since the beginning of time, grandfathers have passed on opinions and ideas to grandchildren to help them progress through life. The author sat down with pen and paper and wrote this book to grandsons and did not refer to any reference materials.

Dedication:

To my grandchildren Bill, Britney, Andrew, Veronica, Colin, Madison, Jackson and all that may follow.

A special thanks to all the Grandpas that preceded me.

Most of all to Glenda, who is my wife, my best friend, my lifelong private secretary, my partner and the love of my life (and she can cook!)

"...ADVICE TO GRANDCHILDREN IS USUALLY WASTED."

Harry S. Truman
33rd President of the United States of America

• *Harry Truman has been in my home and I have been in his.*

• *Harry Truman was left-handed. I am left-handed.*

• *I have even shaken hands with Harry Truman left-handed.*

• *I honor and respect Mr. Truman as a humble and intelligent man.*

*However, in spite of his remark about advice to grandchildren usually being wasted, I believe that **any** advice, whether to grandchildren, children, friends and even enemies, if given honestly and taken in the right spirit, can be helpful.*

It may be true that much advice is "usually wasted" but if anyone reading this book utilizes and gains from just one piece of advise from it, I will feel that I accomplished my goal.

Joe Baker
Author of "Grandpa Told Me..."

CONTENTS

INTRODUCTION

In the mid-1980's I was on a business trip and while on a flight from New York to Los Angeles I started writing some notes to my newly born grandson. I was traveling all over the world at that time and thought if anything happened to me I wanted my new grandson and all my future grandsons to have some of the insights only a grandfather could give. As I wrote I noticed the man sitting next to me was reading over my shoulder. When I started to put my papers away, he asked, "What exactly are you writing?" I explained my notes and ideas to him and he said, "I sure would like a copy of that." And that is how it all started...

Eventually I decided to write, not just to *my* grandsons, but also to those who did not or might not get a chance to know their own grandfathers, and even to those who knew their grandfathers but were not sure just what their grandfathers told them or would have liked to tell them.

That is what Grandpas are for - to tell you about lots of things - to throw out ideas and suggestions so that you can pick and choose what you want to listen to and what you will incorporate into your own life - unlike parents, especially "fathers", who want you to listen to and accept *everything* they tell you.

There are a lot of "do's" and "don'ts" that you constantly get from others (and that will even include me!) However, keep in mind that respect for *others'* rights includes allowing them to speak what is on their minds and that will often require a lot of restraint on your part. The more *self-control* that **you** have will eventually greatly increase the pleasure you will find in your everyday living.

Since there is not much really new in living, it is most likely that most thoughts and ideas listed here have already been expounded on sufficiently by others. However, that does not preclude *me,* a "Grandpa", from getting in my own "two bits" worth of advice. This is now especially true since it is directed to *you* my "adopted" grandson (from your "adopted" Grandpa!)

Every man should have a Grandpa to listen to, and now *you* have that Grandpa, the 'special' someone who will never condemn you for not listening to *all* of his "old timer's" advice.

If you don't agree with everything written here, that's okay. I probably would not always agree with everything you say or do either.

When men don't agree, it does not mean that they cannot be friends. Even though we may not be able to talk with you in person, remember that there are always a lot of Grandpas out there somewhere who really care how you are doing and in a special and mysterious way are pulling for you.

To those who are concerned as to why this is written specifically to grandsons and not to granddaughters, I can only say that it has been said many times before that you should never attempt to explain something that you know little or nothing about. Having been raised with seven brothers and no sisters, my expertise tends naturally toward males.

So, granddaughters, I hope you do get *something* out of these writings, but ask that you respect my ignorance of the workings of the female mind and refer you to the writings of my wife, Glenda, who could be **your** "special" Grandmother. She is an expert mother and grandmother who happens to be the most caring, loving and honest woman I have ever known.

ONE

~

WHAT *MY* GRANDPA TOLD ME

WHAT *MY* GRANDPA TOLD ME...

Coming from an extremely large extended family, much of the conversational remarks and statements in my family (especially during my youth) were made to a 'general' audience.

One of my Grandfathers died when I was five years old, so I don't remember anything he might have told me. I can remember my other Grandfather speaking *directly* to me with *personal* advice only once as I followed him around one afternoon. Even though I was young at the time, I can recall most of the content of that conversation.

My Grandpa Told Me...

■

"Take good care of your feet and always buy good shoes."
(He was repairing a pair of shoes in his basement workshop. He was a piano maker by trade, but was good at several trades.)

■ "Always build things carefully."
(As we checked his progress on some sort of intricate wooden box he was building.)

■

"Eat and drink slowly, especially those things you like the best - you will appreciate them more. This is especially true with black licorice and ice cold beer."
(He gave me some licorice, but never a beer.)

■

These few sentences may not be a lot to hang your hat on, but it's all that I can remember. This Grandfather was one of the finest gentlemen of his era and was known for always speaking well of everyone. I wish that I could relate to you other words of wisdom and common sense, but that's it!

My father raised eight sons who all turned out pretty darned good. This would seem to indicate that what "Dad said" must have had a lasting impact on our behavior.

Since individual time with my busy father was usually at a premium, his "words of wisdom" directed toward me were few and directly to the point. He lived by these rules and taught by good example as well.

To this day I can recall most of the things that MY FATHER TOLD ME...

■

"Treat everyone as your equal, even if you 'think' you might be a little better."
(He grew up in a 'mixed' neighborhood and had many lifelong friends of different colors and backgrounds.)

■

"Always hire the best doctor, dentist, lawyer and accountant you can afford."
(Why settle for second best?)

■

"A man is known by the company he keeps!"
(Don't hang out with someone of dubious character just to have a friend. Too often these people drag you down to their level!)

■

"If you hang out where trouble happens, you will eventually find it."
(And you might just be the one to suffer the most.)

■

"Look it up in the dictionary."
(It's a very interesting and helpful book. To this day I still use a dictionary regularly.)

■

"Use your common sense."
(Your well developed conscience is your best guide.)

■

"Don't drink and drive."
(Don't gamble against the odds of getting hurt or hurting someone else.)

■

"Don't blame someone else for your problems."
(You are the one who makes most of the choices in your life that control your actions - therefore, you have to accept the consequences of those choices!)

■

"Don't try to be something or someone you're not."
(The temptation is always there, fight it and just be yourself.)

■

"Eat what you like and enjoy it."
(Just don't overdo it.)

■

"Respect your tools and weapons and keep them clean."
(It is difficult to do good work with mistreated or dirty tools.)

■

"Respect the rights of others, especially their property rights."
(They worked hard for what they have, so don't mistreat their efforts.)

■

"Take only what you can use."
(This includes just about everything - including eating. 'Waste not - want not' is an old saying but it is still true.)

■

"Always work hard, but don't forget to have some fun, too."
(Take at least one day a week to relax - remember the Sabbath?)

■

"Never miss Church on Sunday."
(Or Saturday or Wednesday. It doesn't make any difference what religion or belief you have, the idea is to keep at it every day of your life. What could be more important? If you pay attention at any religious service, you will learn something of value.)

■

"If you want to stay honest - keep out of politics."
(My father and his father were both deeply involved in politics, so I took their advice. They were unusual in that they both stayed honest and principled men.)

■

"When in doubt, vote those who are in - out!"
(A simple and easy way to keep the life-timers out of office.)

■

"Play the hand that is dealt to you."
(Don't fall into playing the 'what if' or 'if only' hand. Get over it, accept your situation and move on! But remember that you have a 'choice' in how you handle what is dealt to you, so make the right choices!)

■

"Use force only as a last resort."
(My father was one of the strongest men I have ever known. If he struck out, someone was guaranteed to be hurt. His policy was to hold his temper - and he did!)

- "Never stop learning."
(Read! Read! Read! It's not the same as watching television, going to a movie or looking at a computer screen.)

I can't remember exactly just how he said it, but I recall his reminders of "finish what you start". That's a policy we should all remember and implement.

These recommendations alone, if followed, would make anyone into a heck of a man. Yet, I still feel obligated to add what follows as my humble contribution to your legacy. One of the greatest things about your life is that only *you* can decide what type of person you will become. Will you be a happy person? Will you be a friendly person? Will you be outgoing, caring, loving? Others can *influence* the decision, but only *you* can make it!

When you get up in the morning no one in the world can decide whether you are going to be happy or sad. Whether you are going to work hard - or goof off. Not your mother - not your father - not your teacher - not your boss - **NO ONE** decides but **YOU** how you are going to react to the upcoming day! Only you make that decision.

TWO

~

WHAT GRANDPA IS TELLING YOU... **ABOUT YOURSELF**

ABOUT YOURSELF

"Just who in the *heck* do you think you are?"

That is a question that you will be asked someday.

Will you have an answer?

Who are you?

What are you?

Just who *are* you anyway? Well, some things we can be sure of. You are your father and your mother's son! If you live in the United States of America, you are a free man! You have a free will!!! There is no one else in the world and never will be anyone exactly like you - you are a totally unique individual!

You are...the list can go on for pages. We know a lot about what and who we appear to be, but the real test is what we know about the *real* person deep down inside.

The sooner that you find out who you are and what makes you happy, the sooner you can get on with your one and only shot at life - and since anyone who has a Grandpa who cares about him is special; you are, therefore, definitely a very special person.

We should decide as early as possible in our lives just what kind of person we would like to be and then get to work on being just that.

So why not make the right decision now, and then get to work on it - not tomorrow, not next week - NOW!

Take a look in the mirror, see what is there, accept it and then don't waste a lot of time worrying whether you are ugly or handsome, tall or short, slim or fat. You are YOU, and others will just have to accept **whatever** you are, just as you have! When people see that you are comfortable with who you are, it becomes easier for them to accept you as you are.

■

You are what you *want* to be.

■

Try to be yourself .
(Not to be confused with "doing your own thing")

■

You have an *obligation* to do the right thing, so why not do it because that's what you *want* to do!

■

Set your standards high, then don't let anyone knock them down and don't comprise.

■

There is NEVER a good enough excuse for lying, stealing or cheating.

■

When in doubt, *listen*!

■

Listen to what others have to say, evaluate it, but then make up your own mind.

■

Never stay mad or hold a grudge as you will suffer internally for your unforgiving attitude.

■

It's usually better to talk or run than to fight.

■

Never start a fight! Fighting is never a good thing,   but if there is absolutely no getting out of it and if you must strike back - then make them *hurt*.   Fight with every ounce of strength you have. Even if you lose, people will give you space and respect you if you have a certain limit of tolerance.

■

Don't yell at anyone and don't let anyone yell at you.

■

If you are wrong, be brave enough to admit it and learn from your experience.

■

If you are right, don't brag about it or think that you are smarter than anyone else.

■

When you are embarrassed, try not to explain, just smile if you can. Use your 'the joke's on me' smile. It's okay to laugh at yourself and it shows that you are human.

■

When in large groups, classes, meetings, church services, etc. try to remain as quiet as possible as each disruption is magnified, making it harder for others to hear and concentrate and tends to make the gatherings last longer; then, when you do speak - it will get more attention.

■

Live every day as it if were a special one - because it is!
*(You will never get another shot at it and, who knows, it
may also be your last.)*

■

If you make a mess, clean it up...that's ANY kind of mess
- whether you are at home, at work - anywhere!
*(No one wants to live in a mess, so help keep your room,
your home, your school, your car, your city, your world
clean. It's good exercise and keeps the world unclut-
tered.)*

■

Don't try to impress others with your talent, abilities or
newly acquired knowledge.
*(If you have a talent, it will show up without your brag-
ging about it.)*

■

Don't try to act like you know a lot about something you
don't.
*(You will only end up making yourself look like a fool
and from then on people will pay less attention to your
opinions.)*

■

Get organized. You will not only get more accomplished and have more leisure and fun time, but you will be able to find the things you are looking for if you have put them away in their proper place. Make notes with that pen and paper you keep in your pocket. It will help you remember the things you need to do.

(I began my first full time job at a small company that was just getting started. There were hundreds of things to get done and organized. Even at seventeen years old, I knew that I would never be able to remember the dozens of jobs that I was being assigned, plus other jobs I could see on my own that needed to be completed. It seemed natural to me to pull the piece of paper I always carried out of my pocket and make a note on my list of 'Things to Get Done'. It sure helped, as eventually I became General Manager of part of that company and later the President of my own corporation. Little things count!)

■

Lighten up and have some fun!

■

Keep your important papers in a three ring binder, along with other papers you need to keep... like guarantees, instruction manuals, etc.

■

There are some things that need to be kept in a more secure place. For instance, copies of your drivers license (or school i.d.), titles, stocks, wills, bank account information, insurance policies, etc. For this type of item you need to invest in either a safe deposit box at your bank, or a small fire-proof safe to keep at home.

■

Something that helps *me,* is to keep lists of things I want to accomplish. As long as you are going to make a list, a good start is to begin carrying *four* small lists in your pocket:

- A list of everyday jobs to get done (at school, at work and at home).

- A list of fun things to do - places to go and see (see Chapter 9).

- A list of things to accomplish. (Skills I want to learn, etc.)

- A list of things you would like to own someday.

It is very satisfying to pull out your lists, review them, and cross off items you have completed.

Even today, friends will say to us, "How do you get so many things done in a day?" It's easy when you have a list to follow.

■

Be aware of your surroundings.
(Many people get hurt and/or picked on because they are not aware of where they are, where they are going, or what they are doing. Know where you are going, how you are going to get there and what you are going to do when you arrive. If you are leaving a store, a bank, school or the mall, be aware of who is around you and what is going on around you.)

The following pages will give you somewhere to begin your list making. But don't stop there. We always have a list of things we want to get done for each and every day. Sometimes we make them ahead of time and other times we make them as we see things to do.

EVERY DAY JOBS TO DO
WORKSHEET

_____

_____

_____

_____

_____

_____

_____

_____

_____

_____

_____

_____

_____

_____

_____

_____

_____

_____

FUN THINGS TO DO - PLACES TO GO
WORKSHEET

_____

_____

_____

_____

_____

_____

_____

_____

_____

_____

_____

_____

_____

_____

_____

_____

_____

_____

_____

_____

THINGS TO ACCOMPLISH
WORKSHEET

_____

_____

_____

_____

_____

_____

_____

_____

_____

_____

_____

_____

_____

_____

_____

_____

_____

_____

_____

THINGS I WANT TO OWN
WORKSHEET

_____

_____

_____

_____

_____

_____

_____

_____

_____

_____

_____

_____

_____

_____

_____

_____

_____

THREE

~

WHAT GRANDPA IS
TELLING YOU...
ABOUT YOUR BODY

ABOUT YOUR BODY

Your body is going to grow into whatever shape and size it is going to be (pretty much regardless of what you do or don't do) so don't waste too much time worrying about how tall, short, skinny or fat you will be. (This does not mean to abuse your body by overeating or over dieting!)

Just let it develop at its own speed. As you get older, the size and shape of your body becomes of less and less importance since by that time you should have realized that what you are inside is much more important than what you are outside.

■

Keep it clean
(If your body has an odor, you will be the last to know it.)

■

Take a shower or bath daily, if possible.
(It's all right to let your body 'rest' once in a while. But, except for 'resting' on weekends, you should take a daily shower or bath. If you are involved in sports you may need a shower more often - even on weekends.)

■

When taking your shower or bath, start at the top and work your way down to your feet and don't take too much time in the middle.)
(This makes for faster showers and fewer distractions.)

■

It is easier to keep your fingernails clean if you keep them cut to the proper length. Resist the temptation to have your fingernails manicured as they usually wind up looking feminine.
(I still use my Swiss Army knife scissors [that I always carry in my pocket] to cut my fingernails.)

■

Don't forget your toenails.
(Cut them straight across with regular toenail clippers so they don't get ingrown. [The Swiss Army knife won't work for toenails.])

■

If you catch athlete's foot, don't worry about it - just apply an anti-fungal product every day for at least one month and it will clear up.

■

Brush your teeth after breakfast and floss and brush them before going to sleep every day. Your overall health depends a lot on having healthy teeth.
(Have them professionally cleaned at least once a year - every six months is even better. A clean mouth feels good!)

■

Carry a small comb in your back pocket (but not one with a handle that will show by sticking out). Try not to loan out your comb, but if you do - just give it to the person borrowing it and buy yourself another one.
(Why take a chance of getting lice or something from the borrower! Remember small pocket combs are cheap.)

■

Never comb your hair in public - it makes you look vain.
(Use the mirror in the car or bathroom.)

■

Have your hair cut in a way that flatters the way you look.
(Stay away from faddish or hard to maintain styles.)

■

Have your hair cut so you can keep it fairly neat just by running your hands through it.
(If it is cut in a way flattering to you, you will be able to do this and then even if you don't have a comb with you your hair will always look nice.)

■

As you get older, don't attempt to comb your hair over a bald spot.
(It usually looks terrible and doesn't fool you, much less anyone else.)

■

When you first start developing facial hair, don't start to shave until you absolutely need to.
(After you have first shaved a few times, it is not nearly as much fun as you thought it would be, and from then on you must constantly shave for the rest of your life.)

■

If you decide to grow a mustache or a beard, keep in mind that neither is very flattering on the majority of men.
(Consider getting an impartial opinion of how they think it looks on you - and girlfriends are usually not impartial!)

■

Try not to use smelly after shave lotion or colognes.
(If you think you have body order - take a shower!)

■

As you grow older your nose, eyebrow and ear hairs will start to grow wilder, quicker and thicker so begin to check on them periodically and deal with them.
(I once met a man whose nose hairs were so long it looked like he had a mustache.)

■

If you must pick or scratch your nose in front of some-one, turn away from them and use your handkerchief - not your bare fingers.

■

If you feel you must spit or pass gas, do it when other people are not around.
(It is not pleasant for others to hear or see and makes you look uncouth.)

■

If someone is standing around in a public restroom and starts up a conversation - get done and get out quickly! He could be trouble.

■

Do NOT let *anyone* touch your body in private places except your doctor during a physical examination.

■

Sit up straight.
(It not only makes you look more poised, your back will appreciate the extra effort later in life.)

■

When lifting heavy objects, squat down - keep your back perfectly straight and use your legs to lift.
(Your leg muscles are the strongest muscles in your body - use them!)

■

Your gut will start to show more as you grow older, so try to keep your stomach sucked in a little.
(Your control will help your appearance and your muscle tone, but realize that it is hard to hide a large stomach.)

■

Get into the habit of doing a few sit-up exercises before getting out of bed each morning.
(A good doctor or chiropractor can show you which type is best for you.)

■

Plain old walking is the best and least damaging exercise for your body.
(This is your only body so take care of it!)

■

Walk whenever possible! When driving, park your car in an area away from the entrance instead of trying to park as close as you can to your destination.
(Leave the close up parking to the old folks and the handicapped. Besides, you need the exercise more than they do.)

■

Every so often you are going to experience a pain of some kind somewhere in your body. It is usually best just to work your way through it. You can handle most pains and they will usually go away in a short time.
*(If the pain continues after several days, **then** it's time to get professional help.)*

■

Keep your aches and pains to yourself.
(No one really wants to hear about them)

■

Some doctors get rich taking care of 'every day' pain.
*(The really good doctors would prefer that you handle the every day aches and pains yourself and let them spend their valuable time treating your **real** needs.)*

■

Remember - there are good, fair and poor mechanics. Doctors are **body** mechanics - so, just as you would with other mechanics with different skills and work experience, take what they tell you with a grain of salt. (But get the best you can afford and follow his/her advice.) Even the good ones are still learning every day (maybe that's why they are called *'practicing'* physicians) so if you are not sure, don't hesitate to get a second opinion. If that offends the first doctor, you should probably avoid him anyway.
(When I was growing up we probably had only one aspirin a year and all of my brothers and I have grown old in generally good health.)

■

Don't get trapped or talked into getting a tattoo.
(I have yet to meet a grown man with a tattoo who was not sorry he had it.)

■

Sometimes there is a temptation to "get a tan". The fact is that regardless of your skin color you eventually *will* develop skin cancer of some sort if you expose your skin to too much sun.

(If you must be out in the sun for long periods of time, be sure to use a good sun block - especially on your face, nose, ears and the back of your neck and hands as those are the prime areas of danger. Most people will not notice your method of protection.)

FOUR

~

WHAT GRANDPA IS TELLING YOU...
ABOUT EATING AND DRINKING

ABOUT EATING AND DRINKING

You would not put bad fuel in an automobile, so be especially careful what kind of 'fuel' you put into your body.

■

You are what you eat - so try to eat a balanced meal as often as possible.
(No, a hamburger with fries is not considered a balanced meal. It is okay to have those once in a while, but you still need vegetables and a salad thrown in for good measure now and then.)

■

Self-restraint is the best diet. Ease up at the buffet tables - you will not starve.
(I admit that I have attempted to drink dry the 'free refill' soda fountains at fast food restaurants, but have never been successful.)

■

Always wait to begin eating until everyone at your table has been served.
(The wait will be good for your 'patience' training and will make your food taste better - even if it does get a little cold.)

■

If you are with someone who says "grace" before eating, lower your eyes and stay quiet until they finish.
*(It's a good time for you to thank God that you have some-thing to eat - so **you** could be the one saying 'grace'.)*

■

When someone else is paying for your meal, never order the most expensive item.

■

Always order your meat cooked at least 'medium' - that way it will be cooked at least enough to be safe to eat.

■

Never order a whole lobster, corn-on-the-cob or bar-b-qued ribs when out on a date or at a business dinner, as you will most likely make a mess of yourself - or some-one else.

■

It's best to only order bar-b-que at establishments that specialize in hickory smoked bar-b-qued beef.
(Bar-b-que is one of the world's greatest foods, yet it has been some of the worst food I have ever eaten when not prepared properly.)

■

Drink water or iced tea (with lemon) during sit down lunches.
(This helps cut down on the volume of sweet drinks and colas that you can always enjoy after lunch. Plus, it will keep you from having those mid-afternoon 'crashes' in energy.)

■

Never drink hard liquor during your meals.
(In spite of what some will tell you, it does not make good food taste better.)

■

When others order fancy after-dinner drinks, it is okay for you to order nothing, a soda, a beer or whatever you like.
(If you can't think of anything when declining an alcoholic drink, just say you have some things to take care of later - then don't explain your reason any further.)

■

Never drink alcohol when you are working and never before 5:00 p.m.
(If you don't make this your rule, you will sooner or later pay a stiff price.)

■

When going into a drinking establishment that you are not familiar with, don't 'go deep'.
(That is, stay toward the front by the door so that you can retreat quickly if trouble starts.)

■

Don't pick your teeth (or floss them) when others can see you and *never* carry a toothpick around in the corner of your mouth.

■

Eating is one of the purest pleasures in life, but we often get caught up in the trap of "ever more exotic" is better! Sometimes it is refreshing to get back to the simple and basic food and drink that can give us pleasures equal to and even beyond "expensive cuisine".
(A simple hamburger cooked on an outdoor grill tastes great!)

■

At night keep a drink of water at your bedside.
(Often during the night I wake up with 'dry mouth' and having a glass of water close at hand sure helps.)

■

Here is a list of simple things that I like to eat and drink and that you may want to try. Check it out and then make your *own* list of things that **you** like. You will notice that your tastes change as you grow older. Recheck my list after a few years with yours and see how some things taste better and some taste worse:

- Oreo cookies and ice cold milk

- Chocolate chip ice cream in a cone

- Vanilla ice cream covered with chocolate syrup and
     Spanish peanuts

- T-bone steak sprinkled with ground garlic, broiled on
     an open fire and then covered with fried mush-
     rooms

- Hot oatmeal with milk and sliced peaches

- Ice cream on a stick covered in chocolate

- Cinnamon & raisin toast topped with butter, peanut
     butter and then grape jam (part of my breakfast
     for over 60 years)

- M & M's chocolate covered almonds

- Roast beef, mashed potatoes with butter and creamed corn - a meal hard to beat!

- Popcorn, a Coke and a Snicker's bar - especially at the movies

- A handful of almonds with a Hershey chocolate almond bar

- Colby longhorn cheese - eaten like an apple

- A fresh apple and salted crackers

- Ice cold watermelon

- Bar-b-qued beef ribs cooked over a hickory fire until all the fat is smoked out

- Chocolate covered peanuts sprinkled with salt (yes, I said sprinkled with salt - try it!)

- Root beer floats (put a scoop or two of vanilla ice cream in a glass and pour root beer over it.)

- Chocolate ice cream soda made with vanilla ice cream

- Baked sweet potato covered with butter

- Grandma Noni's chili with buttered crackers and ice
   cold Coke
   (See recipe on next page)

■

Every year I add one or two things and every year I take one or two things off my list. Don't let yourself get locked into thinking you have to keep something on your list. Everyone's tastes and likes change as they grow and mature.

■

Grandma Noni's Chili Recipe

(You can make it yourself in about one-half hour)

1 lb. ground beef or turkey or deer meat, etc. (chose one)
1 - 8 oz. can of tomato sauce
1/3 cup chili powder (Grandma Noni considered Wil-
        liams brand to be the best)
1 - 15 oz. can white pinto beans
1 - 30 oz. can chili beans

Brown the meat of your choice in a large Dutch oven
(pan or skillet) until all fat is cooked out or drained off.
Add tomato sauce, chili powder and both cans of beans
with their juice. Cook over low heat for a minimum of
15 minutes. Longer if you like. Serve hot with buttered
crackers and ice cold Coke.

The beauty of Grandma Noni's chili is that you can
change the flavor just by adding things to the basic recipe. Sometimes I throw in a fresh tomato chopped up or
a can of diced tomatoes. Most times I put in a spoonful
of garlic and a small can of mushrooms. Experiment
yourself until you get it just the way you like it.

■

"Grandma Noni" was my mother and she raised eight strong and healthy sons (including me) on her 'special' chili which was served at home every Saturday afternoon. The tradition carries through to my own family today...why not start your own cooking traditions now?

FIVE

~

WHAT GRANDPA IS TELLING YOU...
ABOUT CLOTHES

If you are wondering about the hand-kerchief on the cover of this book, check out Page 79!

ABOUT CLOTHES

■

Clothes do not make the man - but they sure do fool a lot of people.

■

A good sports coat, worn with nice slacks, a long-sleeved shirt with a button-down collar and a tie fits most occasions and allows you enough pockets to carry most of what you need.

■

Except in extreme heat, never wear a short-sleeved shirt with a suit or sports coat.
(In spite of what some fashion 'experts' say, the combination does not look quite right.)

■

Long sleeved shirts should show at least 1/4" of cuff beyond your coat sleeve.

■

When in doubt - overdress.
(You can always remove a tie or jacket.)

■

Do not feel it necessary to dress *down* to what others are wearing.

■

Change *all* your clothes every day and wash the washables, regardless of how long you wore them.

■

Wear clothes that **you** look good in - in spite of the current fad!

■

Never wear tight clothes, pointed toed shoes or shiny suits - they all look bad on men.

■

Never wear a hat or cap inside - it shows a lack of class and manners.

■

Wear clothes made of cotton when possible - the fabric breathes.
(Cotton clothes are usually more comfortable and allows your body freedom of movement.)

■

Check the length of your pants regularly as they have a tendency to shrink and shorten up in the legs.
(With dress slacks, don't let the hem or cuff get too far above the heel of your shoe.)

■

Avoid dark shirts with light ties, it only works in the gangster movies.
(When you are unsure of what colors or styles 'go together', ask any woman and their choice is just about guaranteed to be correct.)

■

Wear loafers when possible and comfortable walking shoes at other times.

■

Wear black socks when wearing black shoes and black slacks, brown socks with brown shoes and brown slacks. Wear white socks for leisure shoes (unless your leisure shoes are black - then wear black socks).
(The exception to this rule is if you are wearing shorts. Don't wear black socks with shorts.)

■

Learn to tie shoe strings, especially on sports shoes, so that they do not easily become untied. Here's how...

Start with a half-knot (that's the first half of a simple 'granny' knot where you just wrap one end through the other). Pull it tight.

Take one string (loose end) and make a loop (Loop 1).

Keep hold of Loop 1 and wrap the other string around Loop 1 and push it part way through the opening under Loop 1 making Loop 2. Leave it loose!

Wrap Loop 1 around and under the string in the middle, push it through the opening above Loop 2 and below Loop 1. Pull both loops tight.

When you are ready to release the knot there is no problem - simply pull each loose end at the same time and it comes untied immediately.

It takes practice to get it right, but it is worth it! When you finally get the hang of tying your shoes this way, you will never again have to worry about tripping on an untied shoe string.

There is probably a name for this knot, but I don't know what it is. The next time you are near a library or book store, check out a book on knots. A few simple knots and hitches will be of great use throughout your life.

■

When dressed, *always* have the following items with you:

> - A clean white cotton handkerchief (every man should carry one - and use it!)
> *(Why do you think your dress slacks and your jeans have **two** back pockets? Obviously one is for your wallet [which you should <u>now</u> carry in your front pocket] and the other is for your* hand-kerchief! *If a man tells you he does not carry a handkerchief and shakes your hand, wash your hands as soon as possible. Many men wipe their runny noses with their right hand and will then shake hands with you. There are few things more disgusting than having someone sneezing and try-ing to cover it with his bare hands or by raising his arm and attempting to sneeze into his sleeve. The sneeze usually goes everywhere! Remember - a sneeze travels at over ninety miles per hour and can travel three to six feet before it settles. That's what your handkerchief is for!)*

- A small pocket knife with a scissor attachment.
(I have always carried a small Swiss Army type knife in my pocket. I can't tell you how often I have used it and other people have borrowed it.)

- Your wallet
(A leather money clip and card case in one piece. You can carry a few credit cards, drivers license, etc. in its pocket and your money in the clip. Carry it in your front pants pocket - not the back - for security purposes.)

- A small ball point pen
(They have these great short 'space' pens now with no pocket clip. One of these can easily be carried in your front pants pocket.)

- A small piece of paper on which to make notes.
(I find 3x5 index cards folded in half work great!)

- A small comb
(Remember! One that does not stick out of your pants pocket.)

- A wrist watch
(I have been gifted several expensive watches over the years and yet today am wearing a simple Twenty Dollar Timex that I can read without my glasses.)

- Enough change for a phone call
(Even if you have a cell phone with you.)

If I had kept track of all the times in the last fifty years that someone has asked me for - my pen, my paper, my comb, my knife, change, or the correct time; I am sure it would be in the hundreds - maybe even thousands.

BE PREPARED! Don't wind up being the 'asker'.

■
Your thin wallet should contain:

- Your i.d. or drivers license.

- A single piece of paper listing important dates clothing sizes (especially your wife's, parents or friends), important phone numbers and addresses. If you are worried about someone getting their hands on the list, put it in code or memorize the important numbers and leave them off.

(Your social security number or bank account numbers should never be carried with you or be on your list.)

- A **maximum** of two credit cards.
 (You should never need more than that.)

- Enough cash to get you home from wherever you are.
(This does not include the money in your money clip.)

- When traveling long distances, at the very least carry enough money in Travelers Checks to get you home.

■

About your pocket knife:
- Always carry a *small* pocket knife and keep the blade clean and sharp.
(Remember, you can't carry it on an airplane or when entering restricted buildings.)

- A good knife man or Boy Scout leader can show you how to sharpen it and keep it sharp.
(If you do not have a sharpening stone available you can sharpen a knife blade on concrete if necessary.)

- Always keep the sharp edge of the blade pointed away from you when cutting.

- A small "Swiss Army" type knife with a 'scissor' attachment is a good choice. They usually contain a toothpick, tweezers and fingernail file along with the ever-useful knife blade and scissors.
(Good things often come in small packages.)

When you are reviewing some of these things and think to yourself "I could never afford that." Always remember that people are looking for things to get you for Christmas, your birthday, graduation, etc. These are the kinds of things you can put on your list that someone would be happy to get you knowing it is something you really want.

SIX

~

WHAT GRANDPA IS TELLING YOU...
ABOUT EDUCATION

ABOUT EDUCATION

■

You can be stripped of all your possessions **except** your integrity and your education.
(They can take everything away from you - your house your car, your possessions, even your family, but they can never take away your integrity or your education.)

■

My third grade teacher let us know that before we finished the year and walked out of her class we would have mastered the basic fundamentals of English, Math and Religion - and then, on that very first day of school, proceeded to show us how we would *accomplish* that goal. We **did** accomplish our goal!
*(I still remember the kids in the other classrooms laughing and playing around. I remember feeling cheated that **we** were starting right in to work on the very first day of school. But the tough training that I received in the third grade was the foundation that made the rest of my education seem relatively easy!)*

■

Don't pass up the opportunity to learn the basics of your education while you are young.
(It is much easier to learn the basics while your mind is open and clear.)

■

Take the hardest required courses as soon as possible so that you can take the easier classes as you get older.
*(Then they **DO** get easier as your education continues!)*

■

Every instructor, every class session, regardless of the subject, has *something* to offer. If you use that approach, you will always be able to pick up something of value that you may be able to use later.
(There will always be teachers that you don't like or that you think don't like you, but hang in there - believe it or not - you can still learn something you didn't know before.)

■

When studying for a course or class, begin by quickly reading the entire text - completely. Just as if you were reading a novel. Then start over by reading it again, *studying* one chapter or section at a time.
(If possible, do this before the course even begins. In this way, you will get an overview and better understanding of the subject at hand.)

■

Minutes before a test, review your list of the items that were the hardest for you to remember.

■

Take class notes in a 'steno' type notebook. They are thin, book size, easy to purchase and easy to carry. Later you can refer quickly and easily through the pages. Use a different notebook per subject (be sure to check and see if your teacher will allow that).

■

Never cheat! If you are having real problems with a subject, let the instructor know why you are having trouble. *(Don't ever be afraid to ask for help from a teacher - that's what they are there for!)*

■

If you are having extra trouble with a subject - try to find someone taking the class with you to review and compare notes.
(Sometimes it helps to work on tough subjects with others...but never copy their answers.)

■

Take courses in Spanish or some other foreign language and become proficient in at least one (besides English) - both verbal and written use. Your job prospects and personal satisfaction will increase dramatically.
(Haven't you always wanted to be able to speak in a foreign tongue?)

■

Get rid of your old books if you must, but keep for future reference the ones you enjoyed the most.
(Later in your life you may find they will come in very handy to refresh your memory about a certain subject.)

■

During your lifetime you will most likely spend more time traveling to and from work than you will have spent in classrooms, so why not consider utilizing that wasted driving (or riding) time by listening to language or instructional tapes while you drive.

■

Control the bad habit of using everyday foul language. It is a very hard habit to break, is unpleasant to hear and magnifies to others your lack of vocabulary and intelligence.
(I do not remember ever hearing either my Mother or my Father use curse words.)

■

Learn to type - others will find it easier and quicker to read your notes and letters. It will make you a more efficient and effective communicator...especially when using computers.

■

When writing, take the time to print or write clearly. *(My own penmanship is not the best, so I always print so people can read what I have to say.)*

■

Develop your own brand of shorthand (or take a class on shorthand at school). It will help you take quick notes for your classes.

ABOUT YOUR READING

Consider your education as *limited* until you have read:
+ Zane Grey - "The Last of the Plainsmen"
+ Jack London - "The Call of the Wild"
+ Mark Twain - "The Adventures of Tom Sawyer"
+ Arthur Conan Doyle - "The Adventures of Sherlock Holmes"
+ Pearl S. Buck - "The Good Earth"
+ Henry Wadsworth Longfellow - "Song of Hiawatha"
+ James Herriott - "All Creatures Great and Small"
+ Charles Nordoff - The Bounty Trilogy: "Mutiny on the Bounty" - "Men Against the Sea" and "Pitcairn Island"
+ One book of your choice by Joseph Wambaugh
+ One book of your choice by Andrew M. Greeley

+ One book of your choice by James A. Michener
   (Give yourself extra time on this one!)
+ One book of your choice by William F. Buckley, Jr.
+ The New Testament from the Bible
   (Most people you meet in your lifetime will have read all or parts of it.)
+ At least five of the fifty plus "Great Books of the Western World".

This list could go on and on, so make up your own list and start working on reading. I have several hundred books left on my list that I still plan to read.

Here again you will find your tastes changing from time to time. Don't be afraid to change your reading list to match your changing tastes. But, don't short change yourself by not spreading your reading wings over time and try a totally different kind of author or story - just to experience a different writing technic or type of story-telling. I add to my list all the time - and I love the feeling of accomplishment when checking off a book I have just finished.

My wife has always been a busy mother and my business partner, yet she has found time to read over 15,000 books. As you can imagine, she makes a fascinating conversationalist.

■

For pleasure AND your *continuing* education, regularly read the following:

+ "Forbes" magazine
+ "American Heritage" magazine
+ "National Review" magazine
+ "National Geographic" magazine
+ "The Wall Street Journal" newspaper
+ Your local newspaper, and
+ At least one book a month

Most of the above publications are available for you to read **"free"** at your local library.

Try to read good *conservative* writing regularly - you don't have to worry about getting the *liberal* and *socialistic* viewpoint, as you will get it from friends, politicians, academians, radio and television news and *most* newspapers. It's the conservative view that is usually closer to the correct one.

Keep in mind that many confused educators and media types will *slant* the facts to fit their own beliefs - especially those that lean toward the liberal 'left'.

Few liberals like to be called 'liberal' but few men object to being called 'conservative'.

SEVEN

~

WHAT GRANDPA IS TELLING YOU...
ABOUT MONEY

ABOUT MONEY

Money is power and cash usually gets you a better deal!

■

Always carry enough cash on you to cover your miscellaneous "everyday" expenses for a week or so.

■

Carry only the *larger* bills ($50 or $100 bills) in your wallet or between your credit card and license in your money clip. Carry the *smaller* denominations in your money clip in your front pants pocket. In this way, as you pay for small items, no one sees just how much money you have and where you are carrying it and it makes for quicker and easier payment for small purchases.

As discussed above, the ideal idea is that instead of carrying a huge wallet in your back pocket, carry a money clip with room for a credit card, drivers license, etc. in your front pocket...you are less likely to have your pocket picked that way.

Most men look like they have a large **growth** on one side of their rear end, but it is usually just a one or two inch thick wallet containing everything they will *never* need.

■

Keep just the bare essentials in your wallet.
(Make a copy of the important items in your wallet and keep the copy at home or in a safe place other than on you. Again, never carry your Social Security card with you on a daily basis. There are very few occasions when you will need to show it to someone.)

■

When traveling, consider taking along a "pad" of new one or five dollar bills for tip and fun money.
*(Make the pad by taking **new** bills you can get at the bank [don't let them put you off - they can get them if you are persistent]. They will be in sequence, so you will be able to keep track easily of what has been spent. Take the back from a regular scratch pad [or any piece of thin cardboard that is fairly stiff] and cut it to the same size of the dollar bills. Clamp the bills to the back of the pad and spread 'padding compound' across the top edge of the pad of bills. You can purchase the padding compound from office supply stores. Once the compound has dried [overnight], take off the clamp and you are in business. You can now 'peel' off one bill at a time. You will always have the correct amount of 'ones' or 'fives' for tips and it will make your tips for service 'special' and you will be remembered.)*

■

Don't carry a hand held purse - it looks feminine.
(You should not be carrying so much junk around any-way and you will eventually lose it or have it stolen.)

■

Don't "wear" your money.
(Expensive rings, watches, chains and clothes only im-press those types of people you should not be interested in impressing anyway.)

■

Pay by cash or check whenever possible and use credit cards sparingly. This helps prevent a 'surprise' (larger than expected) credit card charge total at the end of the month.
(If you start using 'debit' cards you can eventually over-draw your account and get hit with high fees. Banks love people who use debit cards - do you wonder why?)

■

If you use an ATM card - make sure to keep track of your withdrawals and fees.
(Being able to easily withdraw cash from your account often encourages excess spending. Also be aware that if you forget to deduct your withdraw and fees from your account, you can accumulate substantial penalties for

being overdrawn. I used an ATM card only once - just to see how it worked. Then I cut it up and threw it away and have never regretted doing so.)

CREDIT CARDS:

■

Do not own more than one Visa or MasterCard type of credit card and, if necessary for business, an American Express type card.

■

Cut up any other credit card applications as soon as they come to you (usually in the mail) and you won't be tempted to use them.

(Credit card companies are not in business to help you out financially...they are interested in you using their card. The more you use it the more money they make, especially when you reach the point of not being able to pay off your balance at the end of each month. When you don't pay off the balance each month is when the trouble really begins. The interest is high and accumulates quickly - before you know it you are paying double for the purchase you just couldn't live without. If you feel you must have a credit card - use it sparingly and pay it off each month. This keeps you out of big debt troubles and headache and heartache free!)

■

Be **very** selective in giving your credit card number to someone over the telephone and, if possible, never via internet.

■

Never give out your Social Security number unless it is absolutely and totally necessary.
(Some sales people will tell you that it is company policy and that they can't open an account for you, etc. without your Social Security number. If you stick to your guns and refuse to give it, they will usually give up. If they won't, don't open the account there and do business somewhere else.)

■

Down scale your dreams when it comes to spending your hard earned money just to impress someone - it seldom works.

■

If you get to the point where you are paying interest on anything but your home and/or your vehicle, you are probably living beyond your means.

INVESTMENTS:

■

Set aside ten percent (10%) of each paycheck - five percent (5%) for common stock purchases and five percent (5%) for cash savings.

■

Contribute to your church or favorite charity a fixed percentage of your gross income.
(Somehow it always comes back to you. This is called 'tithing'.)

■

Set a goal of how much money it would take for you to live on for a few months and feel comfortable in case everything went wrong financially. Then, spend only what you absolutely must to survive **until** you have that goal amount in cash in the bank. If it becomes necessary later to draw from that cash reserve, then once again do not spend money easily until you have your emergency 'cash hoard' built back up to its original amount.

■

Only the selfish die rich, but you should at least plan ahead for the time you will spend in retirement and, unfortunately, later (perhaps) in a rest home.

■

If an investment opportunity sounds too good to be true
- you can bet that it **IS**!

■

Don't give in to the temptation to speculate with more
than you can afford to lose.
(Investing for the long term is not speculating!)

■

It is easier said than done, but try to never loan money
to friends.
*(If you do, you will most likely eventually lose both your
money and your friend. Tell them that you don't have any
money to spare. Who does? Don't worry about hurting
their feelings, if they had any real feelings for you they
would not be asking you for money.)*

■

Never co-sign a note of any kind, for anyone!
*(There is a good possibility you will wind up paying it
all off.)*

■

Unless you are using cash that you can afford to lose -
do not gamble and resist the temptation to invest with
partners.

■

Purchase a TERM life insurance policy and maintain it long enough to cover your current liabilities and obligations.

(Term life insurance policies normally are less expensive than whole life policies and build no extra value over the years. However, they are simple to own and less complicated tax-wise than full life policies. An honest insurance man can explain it to you further.)

STOCKS:

■

Never invest your money with someone you met on the telephone.

■

When possible, purchase some stock in the company that employs you. The key word is 'some'. If you do not believe in the company that you work for, why are you working there?

(Sometimes the company has a stock program that allows employees to purchase stock at a reduced price - check it out!)

■

Stay away from 'penny' stocks and most 'new' stock issues.
*(A lot of scams start with 'penny' stock issues. With 'new'
stock issues the Pro's usually get there first!)*

■

Regularly purchase stock in companies that make prod-
ucts or service *you* like and use regularly - and sell them
reluctantly.

■

If you are too young to own stocks in your name, have
your parents or grandparents purchase the stock for you
in your name and their name as "joint tenants in common
with rights of survivorship".
*(We regularly do that for our children and grandchildren
and hope this will enrich their 'golden years'.)*

■

With "DRIP" (Dividend Reinvestment Program) programs, you can buy shares of stock directly from the
company you want to invest in. Not all companies have
them, but the companies that do have DRIP programs
will automatically invest your dividends in more stock
for you.
(This keeps your stocks value slowly growing even with-

out you putting in any more money. However, you can also send in money at any time for additional purchases of stock. Hundreds of good American companies have "DRIP" accounts available for individual investors. Stop by your local library or check on the Internet and get the "800" phone numbers. Call and have them send you the simple and proper paperwork - usually just a page or two. It's easy, so get started this year!)

■

If you feel it necessary, get a good, legitimate stockbroker and stick with him - unless he begins to 'churn' your account.

*(Churning is when a broker or service frequently buys or sells stocks for you and, of course, collects a fee each time they sell **AND** each time they buy! Churning only works in the brokerage houses favor - not yours.)*

■

Unless the company you are investing in has a "DRIP" program and will keep the stock certificates for you, when dealing with a broker try to take possession of your stock certificates and keep them in your own safe deposit box at your bank.

■

Do not get involved in 'buying clubs', 'multi-level marketing' or any such type of 'pyramid schemes'. There is a good possibility you will eventually lose your money, your friends and your self-respect.

(Most pyramid schemes are when the scammers use money people give them to invest in usually high-risk projects. They then take later investors money and pay high returns to the first investors, even though no real profit has been made. These types of schemes continue until they finally crash!)

REAL ESTATE:

■

God is not going to make any more land (as I calculate it) so it stands to reason that as a commodity, with a permanently limited supply, real property (land) is always going to be one of the better *long term* investments.

■

Depending on the current tax laws and your income level, purchase your living quarters if the income tax deductions make it favorable.

■

When purchasing a place to live, buy the least expensive home in the area that you like. If you decide to expand or improve it, your investment should retain and increase its value in a greater proportion than the surrounding larger homes.

(Be sure to check out the surrounding areas before you purchase a home, condo or loft. We would always go and sit in our car and watch the activities around the property being considered at different times of the day and night. Drive around the area for several blocks in each direction to get an idea of the neighborhood.)

■

Do not 'purchase' more real estate than you can afford.
(A good licensed real estate broker will never be in a hurry to sell you property. He/she will determine your needs and ability to pay and act accordingly to help you make the right decision.)

■

Beware of real estate partnerships.
*(Carefully check out **all** those involved.)*

There are no " dead-end" jobs!

EIGHT

WHAT GRANDPA IS TELLING YOU...
ABOUT YOUR JOB

ABOUT YOUR JOB

If success is ninety percent luck, why not be in the ten percent who help *create* their **own** luck. Your present job is the best place to **start** your move toward security and satisfaction.

■

On job interviews, dress for success. If you present yourself as clean, neat and well dressed, you will increase your chance of being hired. Employers rarely hire sloppily dressed, unkempt looking applicants.
(This does not mean you have to wear a suit if you are applying at a retail store or fast food outlet. Just wear clean, ironed, nice clothes that you feel comfortable in.)

■

Everyone is nervous to some extent during a job interview, so try to stay calm and not exaggerate your education and previous employment accomplishments (if you have any).

■

Bad first impressions during job interviews can often be offset by checking back later; thanking them for the opportunity to interview and indicating that you want the job and are willing to work hard.

■

If you work for someone, *regardless* of what you are paid, give your employer your best effort each hour, each day. If he does not notice your hard work, someone else or his competitors will.

(It is almost impossible to hide a good employee.)

■

Be satisfied with the pay you receive for doing your job. *(Sometimes a person will be hired after you have been working at a job for a while at a higher wage. Remember that what you are receiving at that time is what you agreed to when you took the job - things usually balance out later.)*

■

Don't let fellow employees make you feel dissatisfied with your job.

(Once in a while another employee may try to make you unhappy in your job - especially if you seem to be enjoying what you do. Sometimes they do this because they are unhappy in their job and don't like seeing you happy. Sometimes they may want your job and know they can only get it if you leave. There can be any number of reasons - just ignore them and keep doing your best!)

■

When someone in business says they will "watch out for you" take it as just a comment and not a promise or a commitment.

■

Don't expect anyone to "take care of you". You must survive on your own efforts.

■

Most of us are not lucky enough to have a business 'mentor' (this is someone who is a trusted councilor or advisor) so become your **own** by watching how others work and operate and emulate their positive actions.

■

Try to arrive at work at least one-half hour early. It will give you a jump on the day and give you time to plan out your work schedule.

■

Periodically be the **last** one to leave work.
(This gives you time to catch up and shows you care about your work - not just the paycheck.)

■

Treat those in charge of where you work with as much respect as you can, remembering that all things come with time and that no one is perfect.

■

Never lose any sleep worrying about someone getting credit for something good that you did, or an idea that you came up with.
(Let others take the credit, your satisfaction will be in knowing that you are the one responsible for the actual work or idea.)

■

Don't seek to advance yourself through false flattery to your boss.
(This is called brown-nosing.)

■

If you are not tired when you go to bed at night, that could mean that you did not work hard enough that day!

■

Learn how and why others do their jobs - someday you may need to know how to do it.

■

Learn as much as you can about the people you are working with, but never get too involved personally with them.

(Someday they may do things that are not right. Someday you may feel obligated to defend them. Someday you may have to fire them, etc.)

■

Learn as much as you can about the company you work for and the business you are in.

■

Assume that you will not retire from the company you work for, but work as though that is the only employer you will ever have.

■

Your present job or business will most likely not be your last, so do the best you can, but lighten up and enjoy it while you are there.

■

Until you do your own job *perfectly,* do not criticize the efforts of others.

■

Keep abreast of what is going on in your field by subscribing to as many magazines that relate to your business as you can afford. If you can't afford them, write to their editors explaining why they should send you complimentary copies.

(You can always check out their availability at the library - for free! Some companies have their own newsletters. Don't just cast them aside - read them and find out what's going on.)

■

Don't get into the habit of regularly "stopping by for a drink" with the boys after work. It's generally non-productive and will cause you more grief than what you will gain.

■

Whatever your job is, do it **better** than anyone has ever done it before.

■

Whenever you get a few minutes to spare on the job, pull out the list that you carry of small jobs that eventually need to get done, *and get started!*

■

Some things are better done in a quiet, relaxed atmosphere, so when this type of work comes up - if possible, take it home (with permission, if necessary) and do it at your leisure. You will get it done quicker and better.

■

Keep a daily or weekly business diary and review your goals and progress periodically.

■

Try to organize your job so that it would eventually be easy for someone to replace you.
(It is possible you may work your way out of a job, but if you were promoted it would be easier to explain your duties to your replacement. Or if you take sick, someone else would be able to easily fill in for you until you can get back to work.)

■

Until you reach middle age, take at least one job related college level continuing education course each year.

■

If you are asked about a work subject that you are not familiar with, don't fake it. Explain the limits of your knowledge and then research the subject later.

■

If for some reason you are unable to *type* a message, then *print* it, as most people have difficulty reading others' handwriting.

■

If you are still in school, your main job is to go to school and do the best you can. If you have a part-time job while you are going to school, don't let it interfere with school, but don't treat your job like a 'dead-end' job. Depending on your attitude, there are very few dead-end jobs. *(No one can hide a good employee whatever menial tasks are assigned to them. Always do the best you can and be proud of what you do. If your full-time job turns out to be menial type work, try to do your job better than anyone has ever done it before. If your employer doesn't appreciate your efforts - his competitors or others will eventually hear about 'that hard working conscientious employee'. Not everyone can be the big boss but everyone has the opportunity to be a superior employee [and who knows - you could become the boss down the line]. Working hard every day makes the hours fly by. When I was young, I often couldn't take time to eat lunch and yet at the end of an 8-10 hour day, even though I would be exhausted, it felt like I had only worked a couple of hours!)*

■
Do not use company facilities, stamps, etc for your personal mail or shipments.

■
NEVER give or take a payoff.
*(Once you do - someone **owns** you.)*

■
Join the "Elite".
(Every group, every job classification has its own 'Elite'. That's the key word 'Elite'. It takes very little extra work and dedication to be in that special group - those who are the best at what they do. If your duties seem to be dull, boring, dead-end, etc., if continuing your education is a drag, then make the effort to make it into something worthwhile. Do your job so good that those who follow you will be judged by your accomplishments. When you do your job well, someone will notice, even if your boss or those you want to impress do not. Someone will appreciate your efforts and the word eventually gets out. After a while of doing your best, you will notice that it takes very little extra effort to do a superior job, and for the effort expended, the satisfaction is enormous! Always do your best every day. It feels good, is the right thing to do and you sleep better!)

■

At work if you regularly have extra time on your hands, ask your boss if there is anything else you can do or learn.

(That is not brown-nosing and it will not only help your day go by faster, but it will give you more knowledge about the company and other facets of the job.)

I have heard this type of statement so many times that I can almost finish the disgruntled employee's sentence for them. "IF I was paid more, I would have done a better job." My reply is, "If you always do your best and stop worrying about the money, you will eventually be paid more."

An old friend of mine often said, "If if's and buts were candy and nuts - we'd all have a Merry Christmas!"

Stop the "if's" and "but's", work smart and hard and things will get better.

NOTES ON JOBS TO GET DONE

NINE

WHAT GRANDPA IS TELLING YOU...
ABOUT RECREATION

ABOUT RECREATION

■

Take some time off regularly for recreation and recuperation.

■

Leave at least one day open each weekend for 'winding down'.

■

Prepare and hang on your wall a list of all the *fun things* you would like to do.
(Remember that list you started back in Chapter Two!)

■

Prepare and hang on your wall a list of all the *places* you would like to see.
(Remember that other list you started back in Chapter Two!)

■

Plan and take a major trip every two to four years.
(Research the area where you live and take short trips during each year. Many of us miss out on the special sights right in our own state.)

■

At some time in your life spend a week or two traveling through the Great Plains and the Midwest.
(You will see a whole different country and a people about which the average travel advisor knows very little.)

■

When flying, chew gum or swallow a lot and yawn as much as possible as your flight ascends and descends.
(This will help keep your ears clear and open. If you have a head cold, take an over-the-counter remedy about an hour before you fly.)

■

Attend at least one major sports game a year at the sports stadiums in your area.

■

Stop by a local park and watch an amateur baseball game.
(It is sometimes more entertaining than a major league game and a lot cheaper.)

■

Fix a complete dinner for someone you like.
(This could be your folks, a friend, etc.)

■

Take an evening educational course on something outside your field about which you have always been curious.

■

See how far you can walk in a day.
(Don't forget to save some energy so you can return to where you started.)

■

Write someone a personal letter at least once a month.
(Not just an e-mail...a real letter with pen, paper, envelope and stamp - the real deal!)

■

Try turning off all your "electronics" for one full day each month. You will be surprised at how much time you will save.
(You can use this time to get some of those things done on one of your lists!)

■

Turn off TV and go to bed early with a good book once in a while.

■

At least once a year, shut off your television set, radios, compact disc, computer games, cassette tapes, etc. and for *one full week* use the time to catch up on your reading and your thinking.

■

Learn to play chess.

■

Learn to play Cribbage.

■

Learn how to play the card game 'Hearts'.
(It's a great game to play with friends and family.)

■

Learn how to play poker.
(Preferably with friends and hopefully just for fun - not big money.)

■

Plant a tree.
*(It is a great feeling to see a tree **you** planted after it has grown to maturity.)*

■

Learn how to swim.

(When swimming, never dive or jump into the water without checking under the surface for obstructions, shallow areas, etc. It hurts when you hit the bottom before you expect it. I once dove into a pool at a major hotel and immediately hit bottom! They had filled the pool with concrete to a 3' maximum depth but had not yet changed the depth sign on the side of the pool, nor had they removed the diving board. For weeks my face looked like mush. No, I didn't sue the motel nor ask for compensation; I am the one who dove in without checking!)

■

Learn how to dance.

(Don't be embarrassed to ask any female of any age to help you. Most will enjoy the opportunity to help. There is one very simple dance step that you can learn in a few minutes. It can be used with ninety percent of all types of music. Place the flat of your right hand in the middle of your partners back. That helps her stay in rhythm with you. Take her right hand in your left hand and take a short step forward with your left foot - then forward and a little to one side with your right foot. Then step back with your left foot followed by slightly raising your right foot [just kind of rock]. The last two steps should be at double speed of the first steps. The rhythm is - one, two,

quick, quick. This method is good for both fast and slow music. Eventually you will match your steps with the rhythm of the music. Good luck!)

■

UH, OH - ANOTHER LIST!

If you get completely bored and you "just don't have anything interesting to do..." call, go by or write your local Chamber of Commerce office and ask for information available for visitors to your area or go to a local hotel or motel and find their rack containing visitor entertainment information. It should be full of literature on places to see and things to do for travelers visiting your area. From these then make a list of the particular things that you would like to see or do. As you complete them, scratch them off the list. Add items as you discover new places to go and new things to do. As you complete your immediate area, branch out further and further into this interesting and fabulous country.

■

Don't buy expensive sports or hobby equipment until you are sure you will continue with that form of recreation. *(In the beginning rent or borrow what you need. With hobbies it sometimes takes a while to see if you really want to continue with it. If you purchased sports equipment and have become 'bored' with it or have 'passed your prime', face up to reality and/or your limitations and donate it so that someone else can get some use out of it.)*

■

Buy a good baseball bat and keep it behind your front door or beside your bed.
(You may never hit a ball with it, but it could come in handy and you will feel safer for having it. I once inter-rupted two men who had broken into my pickup in the middle of the night and were in the process of stealing the truck. I chased them until they jumped into their wait-ing get-away vehicle. I managed to hit their car three times with my bat and still remember how large their eyes looked as they roared off.)

TEN

~

WHAT GRANDPA IS TELLING YOU... *ABOUT POSSESSIONS*

ABOUT POSSESSIONS

Do not become overly attached to your possessions as they can easily be taken from you. Possessions do not make a man!

As you get older, you will find less satisfaction in ***owning possessions*** than in good relationships and ideas.

■

When you feel that need to "own" an animal, just think of the freedom and beauty of that particular species in the wild.
(People who really like animals the most are generally those who do not "own" them [that is, keep them in captivity]. This, of course, excludes "working and guard" animals.)

■

If you do decide to own an animal as a pet - don't neglect it and don't expect someone else to take care of it.
*(If you are old enough to own a pet, you are old enough to accept responsibility for it. This means **everything** - feeding it, grooming it, walking it, playing with it, cleaning up its messes, getting its shots - whatever that pet needs for its well being.)*

■

Don't be a fair weather pet owner and only pay attention to the animal when you feel like it.
(Owning a pet is a huge responsibility and one that should be taken very seriously.)

■

Generally the longer you wait to purchase something, the better quality you will be able to afford - often with better technology.

■

Never make a major purchase the same day that you decide you want it.
(If you can hold off for just a day, you may find that it was not such a good thing to own after all. This also gives you extra time to check out other options.)

■

Avoid going "shopping" unless you have a specific need.
(When you 'wander' around a shopping mall or a store, you are placing yourself at the mercy of expert marketers and will sooner or later be tempted to buy something - even if you don't really need it.)

■

One of the largest purchases that you may make will be a home.

(Check out the area carefully before making the decision to purchase. Home values can go down, but mortgage debt never does. As mentioned before, be sure to check the neighborhood at different days of the week and different times of the day - early morning - noon and evening. Check for noise levels. How are the traffic patterns? Can you get in and out of the neighborhood easily? Is there shopping (grocery store, drug store, etc.) close by? On the weekends is the street clogged with people, cars, etc.? Drive all around the neighborhood and surrounding area to make sure things are as they should be. Be sure this is an area you want to live in since you could be there for a very long time.)

■

The second largest purchase is usually your automobile. Buying cars is like buying a horse, you cannot be sure of what the seller is telling you, so take it all with a grain of salt and do your homework before you go looking. Have an idea of what kind of car you are interest in.

(If you can, know in advance what the going price is for a new car, used car, etc. Don't put yourself at the mercy of the car dealer. They are there to make money - not baby-sit with you!)

■

In spite of what you hear, you are **not** what your car is.
(A nice guy in a clean, older car makes a better impression than a jerk in an expensive automobile.)

■

Think twice before buying a "small" car.
(In an accident the larger automobile usually 'wins'!)

■

If you are an American, a car built in America by an American company should be your first choice.
(Keep in mind the old saying - it is often best to buy 'local' whenever possible.)

■

With your first car plan to drive it until it drops.
(Each day you keep it running means that much more money you can save toward the purchase of your next one. Before I trade them in, I have put more than one hundred twenty-five thousand miles on each vehicle I have owned.)

■

Assume all other vehicle drivers are going to screw up. It will make *you* a more careful driver.

■

When driving, always resist the temptation to show off, especially if someone is watching or riding with you.
(The tendency is to accelerate quicker when starting out, but that is when a lot of accidents happen. Better for someone not to be impressed than to cause injury or death to yourself or someone else. Besides, it saves fuel to accelerate slowly.)

■

Never drive when you are extremely mad, upset or excited.

■

Don't drive with your radio, CD or tape too loud.
(You may not be able to hear emergency vehicles and could be involved in a serious accident - it also makes it difficult to listen for potential mechanical problems.)

■

Don't get too many traffic tickets as you will pay the price later in higher insurance rates and the lack of credibility as a defense witness for yourself if you are ever involved in an accident. It could also limit your ability to get the job you really wanted **AND** you could lose your license!

■

When driving by schools and in cities, slow down and obey the speed limit.
(Naturally you should always observe the speed limit, but especially in these situations.)

■

Driving is a lot like life in general - if you prepare properly for your trip - things generally go a lot smoother.

■

Keep the best tires you can afford on your vehicle. It's like having an extra insurance policy.

■

Don't forget to periodically clean out the inside of the car.
*(No one likes to get into a car full of candy wrappers, soda cans, school books or papers, etc. leaving them no place for their feet **OR** their seat! Vacuum inside the car at least once a month. It is also a safety hazard if something [like a soda can or bottle] would roll under the brake pedal. That happened once when I moved one of our company trucks. It was a terrible feeling to push on the brake and not slow down. The driver of that truck kept it very clean thereafter!!)*

■

Things to keep in the *trunk* of your car:

- A tire gauge. Develop the habit of checking the tire pressure after every second or third fuel fill up.

- On long trips carry a set of radiator hoses and belts - sooner or later they will leak or break and having spares handy will save you lots of time and money. Carry them even if you don't know how to put them on.

- A basic set of tools (in a toolbox or old gym bag):
    Phillips head screwdriver
    Regular screwdriver
    Regular pliers
    Adjustable pliers
    Small combination wrench set
    Roll of electrical tape
    Flashlight - with batteries kept separately
        This helps keep them 'fresher'
    Folding knife

- Enough money for a tow truck service - it may also be used for a tank of gas or a taxi ride home.

- Some rope or heavy string for tying down loads or your truck lid.

- A few bungee cords or tie downs

- A set of road flares - they could be a lifesaver for you or someone else.

- A set of battery jumper cables

- A fire extinguisher

- A roll of paper towels and a spray bottle of window cleaner.

■
Things to keep handy *inside* your car:

- A pen or pencil and small note book

- A paperback book that you always wanted to read but never had the time for.
  (While waiting for someone you will have something to read - but do not read while you are driving or sitting at a stop light.)

- A box of Kleenex where you can easily reach it

- A map of the area you are in and one of where you are going.

- A litter bag
   *(Don't throw **anything** out the window. You are one of us who eventually must pay for someone else to pick it up.)*

- A handful of change for parking meters, tolls, parking fees, etc.

■

Keep your windshield clean on the *inside* as well as the outside.
(Remember, this is the way you see the world. Make it a clean one!)

■

In case of an accident - remain as calm as possible. If there are no injuries, get the name, address, phone number, and insurance company name, phone number and policy number of the other driver. Also make a note of the car license number, color, year and make of the car, It would be a good idea to make a note of the damage to each of your cars as well. In case of an injury, call 911 immediately.
(The other party will want your information too, so be prepared to have that information at hand.)

ELEVEN

~

WHAT GRANDPA IS TELLING YOU...
ABOUT FAMILY

ABOUT YOUR MOTHER

Maybe hearing this from someone else will make a difference, maybe not, but it is a fact of life that no one else will ever care for you in the *special* way that your mother does.

She carried you inside her for almost a year and it could not have been a particularly pleasant experience for her. She hurt a lot having you and after you were born her body was never the same.

You are one of the reasons for her stomach being a little larger than she would like, her tired legs, her bad bladder and her feeling that she may have missed out on something in life - yep! because of *you*.

This, however, is no reason for you to feel "guilty" as you did not get her pregnant.

To say you are to blame for some of her problems is not correct. You may be the **reason** for some of her problems and trials, but you are also a reason for her fulfillment in the natural evolvement of her life as a female - the giving of life to another, the carrying on of a species. You are also the reason that she can love so deeply as only a mother can.

■

Regardless of what you will do or not do throughout your life, your mother will continue to care for and love you as no one else can imagine.

■

By the laws of nature, your mother must keep up the reminders to you about the quality of your habits, friends, clothes, etc. Take it as good advise as she is doing it for your own good.

■

She does not interfere in your life just to be nosey; it is just that she cares about you in her own special way.

■

Generally a mother expects little and offers *everything*.

■

You have little to offer your mother, but small gestures like a hug, a kiss, or even a note can mean a lot to her. Even if you feel clumsy in giving her a hug or a kiss - keep trying - you must give back some of the love that she so lavishly gave to you when you needed it.

■

Never raise your voice in anger at your mother, you will regret it the rest of your life.

■

When you are with a female of *any* age, make sure to open doors and let them enter/exit first. It's a common courtesy and a sign of respect.
(This means the door to a car, house, restaurant, church, etc. and yes, this even means your sister!)

If she is still alive, write your mother a note or letter - NOW!

ABOUT YOUR FATHER

■

Well, nobody ever said a father had to be perfect. There are not many good "training" programs on how to be a good Father.

■

Don't criticize your father until you have lived as long as he has.

■

You may feel that no man could be good enough for your mother, but then we all compromise a little at some time in our lives.

■

Your father is your father and is what he is. The sooner you accept that fact the sooner you can go on with your life and possibly find him to be almost a friend.

■

Because he lives in the **real** world, when you are young he will never be able to spend all the time with you that you feel you deserve. This has nothing to do with his caring about or loving you; it is just the way things are in real life.

(Usually fathers are out in the world trying to make a living to take care of their families and that is why they are not able to spend as much time with the children as they would like to. This is usually not their fault - so give them some slack.)

■

Deep down inside fathers wish the best for their sons and hope that the sons suffer less than the fathers did as they go on through life.

■

Most fathers do not spend a lot of time telling their children how much they love them. Unfortunately, most fathers do not know just exactly how to do that and they hope their son will come to the correct conclusion (that , in fact they do love them) sooner or later.

■

All sons regret some parts of their relationship with their fathers, especially after he has passed on. Don't wait too late to make him aware of your feelings or appreciations.

■

All fathers regret some parts of their relationship with their sons, especially after the sons leave home.

ABOUT YOUR BROTHERS AND/OR SISTERS

■

If you have brothers and/or sisters, tolerate them and their idiosyncrasies, keeping in mind that someday you will regret the missed opportunities of getting better acquainted with them.

■

Don't expect your siblings to be any better than you.

■

A brother or sister can be a best friend.
(I am assuming that a sister can, as I never had one.)

■

As you grow older, it will be easier to see the basic good in them.

■

Be the one refuge that they can turn to when all others fail them.

■

Sooner or later you must love, defend and forgive your brothers and/or sisters, regardless of what they say or do, so try to accept them for what they are and make your relationships with them happy ones.

■

Some people are blessed with several brothers and/or sisters. Others are the only child. If you are lucky enough to have a brother or sister, cherish them always.

■

All men wish that they had a brother. All men wish they had a good friend. I had seven brothers and they have always been my friends.

(We agree and we disagree, but we continue to love each other because we are brothers and friends.)

On the next page you will find a poem I wrote to my brothers several years ago.

MY SEVEN BROTHERS

by Joe Baker on 03-11-97

If asked "back then" about my true druthers,
I may not have asked for my seven brothers.

But fifty years later if you asked me again,
I wouldn't think twice, and might ask for ten.

It's impossible to duplicate or take away,
The fun we had both in work and in play.

Remembering "back when" is now a treasure,
Very few things can bring so much pleasure.

Memories happy, memories sad - some smiles
and some tears,
Those parties, those trips, those too many beers.

The runs in the woods, climbing the trees,
The fights, the sunburns, the scrapes on the knees.

The BB gun fights, the king of the hill,
The thrill of the hunt on the first "spatzie" kill.

Dad's deciding to send us to military school,
Proved beyond doubt - he was nobody's fool.

The marches, the parades, the long bus rides home,
Then off to careers, on land, sea and foam.

We're lots older now, getting slower and tired,
Now a lot more pains and too old to be fired!

We have grown kids here and grandkids there,
We're just a tad worn, "Hey, Pops, have a chair!"

Boys, I'll think I'll skip the touch football game,
My time is now past for the sports Hall of Fame.

It's time now to sigh and just kick back,
Let the young be the ones to get their heads cracked.

So to Dad and Mom, I say thanks for my brothers,
Now it's time for a nap - so please had me the covers.

I'll rest quietly now, with no need to shout,
That my brothers love is beyond any doubt.

Maybe it's time to forget your life's fashions and trends,
and make friends of your brothers - and brothers of your
friends!

TWELVE

~

WHAT GRANDPA IS TELLING YOU...
ABOUT FRIENDS

ABOUT YOUR FRIENDS

■

As my father said, "A man is known by the company he keeps."

■

As you can influence others, your friends can influence you, so be careful whom you chose for your friends.

■

Remember that **no one** on this earth feels that he has enough *true* friends.

■

A *true* friend will never ask you to do something that is wrong.

■

There are different kinds of friends - school friends, work friends, neighbor friends, sports friends, church friends, etc. It is sometimes best to keep them separate.

■

To keep a good friend, don't spend **all** your time with him.

■

A good wife can also be your ***best*** friend.

■

Don't let anyone "buy" your friendship...and don't "buy" anyone else's friendship.
(Gifts are great to receive, but they must come to you and be given by you with no strings attached.)

■

Never sell your friends anything - if you can avoid it.
(Sometimes that is the fastest way to lose a friend.)

■

Don't loan money to friends.

■

Don't borrow money from your friends.

■

Have better friends than enemies.

■

Most of the time someone is watching you, so try to set as good an example as you can.

■

Never base your judgment of another on what someone else says about them. Make up your own mind.

■

Almost everyone **older** than you has advise of value to offer you, so respect them at least for that.

■

Always try to call ahead before dropping in to visit someone.
(Giving a warning of your unexpected visit is always appreciated.)

■

You would like to be treated with consideration when you visit someone, so put your own guests wishes above your own.
(It's usually for only a short time and it feels good to be a good host.)

■

Clean your whole house or apartment, but especially the kitchen and bathroom areas, before having a party.
(Many of your guests will spend much of their time in one of these two places.)

■

Have fewer chairs than you have guests.
(This will keep them moving, rotating and mixing.)

■

When you don't know what to say to someone or how to make small talk, ask whoever you are conversing with something about themselves. How are they doing, where do they go to school or work, etc. You will learn a lot this way and they will enjoy 'talking' to you.

■

Never let someone leave your residence without you walking them to the door or car, etc.
(This is common courtesy and lets your guests know you are glad they came.)

■

Never let guests leave if they are intoxicated and planning to drive.
(The inconvenience of caring for them overnight or making sure they get home safely [whether you take them home - if you haven't been drinking - in a cab - or some other designated driver takes them home] is small compared to the chance of them injuring themselves or someone else.)

■

Never be the last one to leave a party, even when you are having a great time!
(Good hosts never like telling their guests that it is time to go.)

■

Friendship is a two way street. Don't expect friends to do all the calling or planning. To be a true friend you must do your share.
(Call, e-mail or write to them regularly.)

■

You should know at least as much about your friends as they know about you.
(Fill out the next page and compare it with your friends/ spouse's list.)

YOUR NOTES

GETTING ACQUAINTED
WITH THE ONES CLOSEST TO YOU

ITEM	YOUR FAVORITE	YOUR LEAST FAVORITE	YOUR FRIENDS FAVORITE	YOUR FRIENDS LEAST FAV
Ice Cream				
Cold drink				
Hot drink				
Cereal				
Restaurant				
Fast Food				
Color				
Movie				
TV program				
Sport				
Relaxation				
Exercise				
Magazine				
Writer				
Vacation				
Vehicle				
Job				
Best Talent				
Weakness				

THIRTEEN

~

WHAT GRANDPA IS TELLING YOU...
ABOUT MARRIAGE

ABOUT MARRIAGE

To marry or not to marry is one of the greatest decisions you will ever make.

If your decision is to stay single your life will move in many directions different from the way it would be if you decided to marry.

Whether married or single, appreciate the advantage of your choice and be satisfied with its benefits.

Some of the happiest and well-adjusted men I have ever met have been single their entire life. Granted, had they ever married, they would most likely have been the same.

■

If you decide to get married, try to pick someone from your own station or level in life and she may be more apt to stick with you during both the good times and the difficult times.

■

Do not get married until you have known your future wife for at least a year.
(You will find out a lot about each other in twelve months.)

■

If you are casual about pre-marital sex, you will never have someone love you without some reserve - they will always wonder about your commitment.

■

The greatest gift a man can give to his wife is his virginity.
*(It's not easy, but it's worth the respect you will have for yourself **and** from her.)*

■

Remember that females are smarter than you, but when they are young - don't forget that in some things they lack common sense.

■

If a girl wears a lot of perfume when she is young, she will most likely gag you with larger amounts of it when she gets older.

■

Don't expect your wife to like everything you like.

■

If you have arguments with your girlfriend while you are dating, don't expect **not** to have them after you are married.

■

Understand that you will have arguments after you get married. After a disagreement, stay calm and don't do anything drastic. Few of us can stay mad long. Better yet, find a way to at least keep talking to each other.

■

Never criticize your wife, as they may forgive - but they seldom forget!

■

When you buy your wife a gift, don't let your feelings get hurt if she doesn't like it.

■

When you really want to do something or get something but your wife does not agree, forget about it and get or do something for her instead - her joy will surpass the fleeting happiness you would have had in getting what you wanted.

■

Give your wife the special gift of being faithful to her. It helps make up for the times you forget her birthday, special moments, anniversary, etc. and she may return the favor.

■

Keep telling your wife that you love her - she needs to hear it often from you.

■

Try to get in the habit of walking with your wife.
(You may have to walk more slowly in the beginning in order to give her time to build up her stamina.)

■

Remember - you should always walk on the curb side when walking with a woman. This protects her from splashes and other dangers.
(This means your mother, sister, aunt, grandmother, etc. as well as your girlfriend and later your wife.)

■

Try to spend as much time with your wife as possible. She can be the best friend you could ever have.

■

When taking your wife to a party, remember whom you arrived with and spend time with her if she appears bored or ignored.
(Be especially aware of this if she does not know anyone else at the party.)

■

When she asks how she looks, tell her the truth so she does not go out and embarrass herself.
(Be careful to break the news as easily as you can.)

■

ALWAYS be as honest as you can with your wife and she should do the same with you.
(You cannot build a healthy relationship without honesty.)

■

Assume your wife must be someone special because she picked you for her partner and treat her that way.

■

Be extra patient while your wife passes through her special physical and sexual stages in life.
(You will have them too, they just are not as obvious in men as in women.)

■

When I got married my father's only advise to me concerning 'sex' was "be gentle!"

FOURTEEN

~

WHAT GRANDPA IS TELL YOU...
ABOUT RELIGION

ABOUT RELIGION

■

If you lie - others will lie.

■

If you cheat - others will cheat.

■

If you steal - others will steal.

■

If you do any or all of the above - no one will ever trust you.
*(Once trust is lost, it is **very** difficult to gain it back and usually takes a very long time.)*

■

Those who say that we should never argue about religion or politics are usually insecure about their own beliefs.
(Besides - it's a lot of fun and educational!)

■

Never downgrade another person's beliefs; it is disrespectful and presumptuous.

■

Respect others' beliefs, even if they seem unusual.

■

If someone must shout his religious beliefs, you can assume that he is wrong.
(When you are confident about your beliefs, you don't have to raise your voice when talking about it.)

■

Don't try to convert the whole world to your beliefs, let your everyday actions speak for you.

■

Never give your Church less than you can afford.

■

If someone tells you "I never go to church", you can assume that he is most likely either self-centered or mentally and physically lazy.

■

Don't put yourself in a position to be dragged down to the moral level of others.
(You do not have to always be "one of the boys". Later you must be able to live with yourself.)

■

Others will tell you about the wild things they do or have done, but remember that most men exaggerate at some time about their 'so called' adventures.

■

When raising or lowering the kneeler in churches that have them, do it quietly. Respect is a key word when around others.

■

Don't be part of the group that stays toward the back of a church during services. On the other hand, don't be one of those who practically trample others in their stampede to be the first to leave.

■

It's okay to be a *little* prejudiced - we all are to some extent.
(Admit it, but try to contain your feelings and opinions as they will usually change for the better as you grow older and wiser. Your distain will usually turn into acceptance and hopefully support for those you originally may have thought so little of. We often find ourselves prejudiced against the new and unknown. For example, when new 'groups' or 'foreigners' move into an area, they do in fact 'behave differently'. They like different foods, life styles and especially seem to have trouble adapting to the living and driving habits of the locals. Keep in mind that you would find yourself in the same situation if you were dropped into the middle of a foreign country.)

■

The prejudice you *really* have to watch out for is your prejudice toward people who are ignorant, arrogant or greedy.

(You have some of these traits deep down in yourself, so be patient as you can with others. They seem less disgusting in time.)

■

Do something good for someone and never let them or *anyone else* know that you did it. It's a good feeling to carry around with you.

(God sees what you have done - and that is all that is important.)

■

Do not be a man who leaves his morals at home.

■

Be a "giver" - not a "taker".

YOUR NOTES

Didn't vote? Can't complain!

*Before you complain about politics -
remember, somebody has to do it.*

FIFTEEN

~

WHAT GRANDPA IS TELLING YOU...
ABOUT POLITICS

ABOUT POLITICS

■

When in doubt about political candidates, consider voting *against* the incumbent.
(If they have not done the job well enough to gain your confidence, vote them out and give someone else a chance.)

■

If you vote for a lawyer, expect to have more laws **AND** more law suits.

■

The more laws we have, the less freedom we have.

■

Beware of candidates mostly supported by academicians or unions.
(Or other so called "interest" groups.)

■

When you assume that it is the **elected** politicians who are at fault for problems; in fairness, it is often the **bureaucrats** who are really to blame.
(A 'bureaucrat' is not elected - they are often appointed and usually have a lifetime job. At least a 'politician' is elected and usually more responsive to the voters.)

■

There must be some honest politicians, but I have not met many lately.

■

Like compulsive shoppers, bureaucrats and politicians will spend whatever money you send them through your taxes.
(They seem to always find it necessary to build larger and larger bureaucracies.)

■

A local politician with real ambition will usually wind up freely spending tax money on projects outside his local jurisdiction.

■

Beware of a governmental employee who is doing something "for your own good" or "for the good of the children".

■

Be sure and do your homework on each candidate so you can make an informed decision before you vote.
(Don't take one person, one TV station, or one newspapers ideas as your own. Get a mixed review of all sides and be truly 'informed'.)

■

There is never a good enough excuse for not voting, so vote whenever given the opportunity - this means both national and local elections.
(Like most people you will usually appear to be ignorant, selfish and lazy when trying to explain why you did not vote. Remember, if you don't vote - you have no right to complain about the way things are.)

■

A regulation that was not voted on by the people will usually turn out to be a bad one.

■

If you feel that the system of government in the United States of America is not the best, read your history, and the current worldwide news. You will find that it sure beats anything else tried so far.

SIXTEEN

~

WHAT GRANDPA IS TELLING YOU...
ABOUT DEATH

ABOUT DEATH

■

Stay in the background at funerals, you may be needed to help behind the scenes.

■

Don't make an emotional scene at funerals. The family already has enough to contend with without being distracted by you.

■

Always keep a dark suit or sports coat handy to wear to funerals. Never distract mourners by dressing festively at funerals.
(True, a funeral is a joyous send off to the loved one who has died, but it is not the time to dress gaudily.)

■

Try to have a get-together with relatives and friends after a family funeral.
(This helps leave everyone on an 'up' note and may be the last time many of those attending will ever get together again.)

■

Don't leave flowers at the grave site, give them to someone living who can appreciate them.

■

Have the simplest and least expensive funeral for your-self and those for whom you are responsible.
(Humility is a wonderful virtue.)

■

Don't leave large monuments behind commemorating yourself. You are special, but not *that great* as compared to some others.

■

When you need a quiet place to think, go to a church or cemetery - most people will not bother you at either place.
(You'd be surprised how quiet and peaceful either of these places are when you want time alone.)

■

Try to leave this world without too many complaints - no one wants to hear about your pains and problems.
(Even when they ask "How are you?" That is a courtesy question and should merely be answered with "Great!" or "Fine!", etc.)

■

Don't die without a will and leave legal problems behind for your heirs.
(A good lawyer can help get it done correctly.)

■

When they are 'dying' there are very few atheists.
(I have noticed that when a so-called atheist is in deep trouble [or dying] they usually ask God for help.)

■

It is best not to mouth off about your lack of beliefs or skepticism about religion because at the end of your life you may be wanting to make your peace with God.

■

Until your children can make it on their own, carry enough life insurance on yourself to cover their upkeep and education in case you would happen to pass away.

■

Do not make plans to leave your grown children too much money or too many possessions. It could mess up their lives while they wait for you to die.
(If you want to give them something, give it to them while you are still alive and can enjoy it with them.)

Now, before *you* 'kick off' how about you sitting down and writing a letter to your future grandsons telling them about **you**! How you feel about things, who you are and what you did with your life. Regardless of your writing ability, no one will ever be able to do it better and no gift would be greater!

SEVENTEEN

GOODBYE...
AND HELLO

GOODBYE...AND HELLO

Sometimes we get the feeling that the way things are going in this old world that there is just not that much to feel good about.

But, when you stop to think about it, there are only a few things that we don't like - but a whole lot of things to feel good about and things that we can really like and enjoy.

I can get a good feeling inside by just thinking about some of the things I like - so now I would like you to make...yes, another list!

This time it is a list of "THINGS *YOU* LIKE".

To help you get started, I have prepared a list of just some of the things I like. (Make up yours and compare it with mine. I hope there are a few things we both like, but keep in mind that we are all different and only you know what makes you feel good!)

Let's see how many things on your list and my list are the same.

THINGS THAT "I" LIKE

■

Windsor knots in ties.
(Can you tie one?)

■

100% cotton clothes.
(They are comfortable and you can easily wash them.)

■

Button down collars on shirts.
(Even without a tie you will always look 'dressed'.)

■

Sports coats with a single vent in the back.
(Your butt will not look like it is sticking out - as it does with double vents.)

■

Dress slacks or jeans that are comfortable, inexpensive, washable and easy to keep clean.
(You do not have to buy the most expensive ones to look nice. Clean is the key!)

■

Zip lock plastic bags.
(Always carry several in your travel bag for socks, wet things, etc.)

■

Soft voices.
(Kind of nice to hear once in a while.)

■

Quiet people.
(The world needs a few of them.)

■

Clear skies.
(There is still hope.)

■

The Rocky Mountains.
(See them to believe.)

■

The Missouri Ozarks.
(Unassuming, but beautiful reality.)

■

Old folks telling stories.
(It must have been a real adventure 'back then'.)

■

People who are NOT 'aginers'.
(The world needs positive doers.)

■

Slow dancing with my wife.
(Reminds me how gentle and adaptable females are.)

■

The smell of an outdoor camp fire.
(Nothing like it.)

■

Hickory 'smoked' beef bar-b-qued ribs.
(Ummm good!)

■

Getting hugged.
(With a 'real' hug. My family members believe in even man-to-man hugs. There is nothing feminine in a bear hug.)

■

Climbing.
(Gives a different perspective to both the climber and watcher.)

■

Walking slowly.
(We miss so much of life - even by walking too fast.)

■

Discovering new things.
("Well I'll be darned!")

■

Reading for pleasure.
(God's gift to the busy man.)

■

Intense discussions - some call it 'arguing'.
(Sometimes it's the only way to quickly cut through the malarkey and get to the truth.)

■

Planting things.
(It's a thrill to see what you planted grow but it does hurt a little to see them die.)

■

Completing jobs.
(Gives you many levels and kinds of good feelings.)

■

Having my back scratched.
(Need a man say more?)

■

Back rubs.
(Ditto)

■

Money in reserve.
(Takes some of the 'worry' pressure off.)

■

Good friends.
(They always understand and don't condemn.)

■

Old religious nuns.
*(An everyday lesson in **real** commitment and humility.)*

■

Happy people.
(They make me happy.)

■

Honest children.
(Will make the world a better place.)

■

Old folks.
(No one knows it better!)

■

Kissing babies.
(They smell and feel good.)

■

Receiving personal letters.
(Always a pleasure and very rare these days.)

■

Honest smiles.
(You can spot them a block away.)

■

Grandkids
(Everybody is one, which means that we are all in this project together and they remind me to be more understanding of others.)

Every year I add one or two things and every year I take one or two things off my lists. Don't let yourself get locked into thinking you have to keep something on your lists. Everyone's tastes and likes change as they grow and mature!

Well, Grandson, it is time to cut this off, but I *still* have two LAST REQUESTS.

Again, regardless of your age, someday soon I would like for YOU to take the time to sit down in a quiet spot and write **your** future grandsons that letter about **yourself.** You can leave them something worth more than all the money in the world.

Second - remember that you really are *special* - so, always keep your chin up and enjoy life - it can be an exciting and fun world out there if you want it to be...so go for it!

Rest assured that I and all the other Grandpa's will be out there somewhere cheering for you!

So, go on out there, be safe and have a good time but, remember our old family saying, *"don't do anything stupid!"*

Goodbye, and...Hello!

YOUR NOTES

EIGHTEEN

~

ABOUT THE AUTHOR

ABOUT THE AUTHOR

JOE BAKER WAS BORN IN KANSAS CITY, MISSOURI IN 1935.

HE MARRIED GLENDA IN 1956. THEY RAISED FIVE CHILDREN AND AT THE PRESENT TIME HAVE SEVEN GRANDCHILDREN. THEY ARE RETIRED AND NOW ENJOY LIVING IN THE BAKER FAMILY HOMESTEAD IN MISSOURI.

HE GRADUATED FROM DE LA SALLE MILITARY ACADEMY AND WHILE HE NEVER SPENT A "DAY" IN COLLEGE; HE DID, IN FACT, GRADUATE FROM DRURY UNIVERSITY BY ATTENDING ALL EVENING COURSES OVER A TEN-YEAR PERIOD.

DURING HIS FORTY-FIVE YEAR 'BUSINESS' CAREER IN THE HEAVY CONSTRUCTION EQUIPMENT BUSINESS, HE MANAGED AND OWNED EQUIPMENT DEALERSHIPS AND MANUFACTURERS AGENCIES; HE TURNED MANY TROUBLED COMPANIES INTO SUCCESSFUL AND PROFITABLE BUSINESSES; HE WAS A MAN-

AGEMENT CONSULTANT FOR OTHER COMPA-
NIES; HAS BEEN AN EXPERT TRIAL WITNESS;
HE HAS TRAVELED EXTENSIVELY; AND, AS A
WAY OF PAYING BACK FOR ALL THE MANY
GOOD YEARS HE ENJOYED BEING IN BUSI-
NESS, HE HAS WRITTEN MANY ARTICLES FOR
VARIOUS BUSINESS PUBLICATIONS.

IN THE 1980'S HE WROTE A LETTER TO HIS
GRANDSONS (WHICH EVENTUALLY TURNED
INTO THIS BOOK FOR ALL GRANDSONS - EV-
ERYWHERE!)

A Note from the Author

I hope you have enjoyed reading "Grandpa Told Me..." as much as I had writing it.

I am now working on a fictional series that will be getting into print shortly. Look for these "Phil Brown" series titles coming out soon.

Black and Blue Brown
Brown & Served

If you would like to order additional copies of *Grandpa Told Me...* either fill out and send in one of the order forms in this book, or contact us at the address listed below.

If you would like to be on our mailing list, send your name, address and e-mail address to:

Joe Baker & Associates, Inc.
Publishing Division
539 Tennessee Avenue
Independence, MO 64053-1134

OR to our web site: joebakerandassociates.com

Joe Baker

DO YOU HAVE A FRIEND THAT YOU THINK WOULD ENJOY READING "GRANDPA TOLD ME..."?

TO ORDER ADDITIONAL COPIES OF

"Grandpa Told Me..." by Joe Baker
Send $14.95 (plus postage of $3.00 each)
for EACH book ordered to:

Joe Baker & Associates, Inc.
Publishing Division
539 Tennessee Avenue
Independence MO 64053-1134
www.joebakerandassociates.com

Date:_____   Check No. _____

(Pay Pal & Credit Cards accepted through our website)

Please send _____ copy(s) of "Grandpa Told Me..." to:

Name:_____

Address:_____

City:_____State:_____Zip:_____-_____

Quantity: _____ book(s) @ $14.95 each = _____

Shipping/
Handlng: _____ book(s) @ $3.00 each = _____
(Continental USA only - contact us for outside USA)

Total Amount Enclosed: _____

Form GPA-808

TO ORDER ADDITIONAL COPIES OF

"Grandpa Told Me..." by Joe Baker
Send $14.95 (plus postage of $3.00 each)
for EACH book ordered to:

Joe Baker & Associates, Inc.
Publishing Division
539 Tennessee Avenue
Independence MO 64053-1134
www.joebakerandassociates.com

Date:_____   Check No. _____

(Pay Pal & Credit Cards accepted through our website)

Please send _____ copy(s) of "Grandpa Told Me..." to:

Name:_____

Address:_____

City:_____State:_____Zip:_____-_____

Quantity: _____ book(s) @ $14.95 each = _____

Shipping/
 Handlng: _____ book(s) @ $3.00 each = _____
(Continental USA only - contact us for outside USA)

Total Amount Enclosed: _____

TO ORDER ADDITIONAL COPIES OF
"Grandpa Told Me..." by Joe Baker
Send $14.95 (plus postage of $3.00 each)
for EACH book ordered to:

Joe Baker & Associates, Inc.
Publishing Division
539 Tennessee Avenue
Independence MO 64053-1134
www.joebakerandassociates.com

Date:_____ Check No. _____

(Pay Pal & Credit Cards accepted through our website)

Please send _____ copy(s) of "Grandpa Told Me..." to:

Name:_____

Address:_____

City:_____State:_____Zip:_____-_____

Quantity: _____ book(s) @ $14.95 each = _____

Shipping/
Handlng: _____ book(s) @ $3.00 each = _____
(Continental USA only - contact us for outside USA)

Total Amount Enclosed: _____

Form GPA-808